Wasting Time

ILLUSION VERSUS REALITY

By Ruby Larry

Copyright © 2018 by Ruby Larry

All rights reserved. This book or any portion thereof may not be reproduced or used in any manner whatsoever without the express written permission of the author, except for the use of brief quotations in a book review or journal.

CONTENTS

DEDICATION ii
ACKNOWLEDGEMENTS iii
INTRODUCTION..iv
CHAPTER 1: WASTING TIME 1
CHAPTER 2: ILLUSION VERSUS REALITY..9
CHAPTER 3: DECISION MAKING, DETERMINE YOUR DESTINATION 27
CHAPTER 4: THE MIRROR AND REALITY 31
CHAPTER 5: TRUTH IS REALITY..38
CHAPTER 6: ILLUSION CREATES YOUR REALITY 46
CHAPTER 7: SEED TIME AND HARVEST...63
CHAPTER 8: BLURRY VISION 70
CHAPTER 9: SPIRITUAL DEATH..76
CHAPTER 10: GUARD YOUR HEART...84
CHAPTER 11: THE ADVERSARY 90
CHAPTER 12: FROM THE INVISIBLE TO THE VISIBLE 98
CHAPTER 13: HOW DO I WIN THE FIGHT AGAINST THE ENEMY? ...110
CHAPTER 14 THE STORM: 115
CHAPTER 15: DREAMS 120
ABOUT THE AUTHOR...122

DEDICATION

I want to first thank God, for making this possible for me. He has used my journey as a personal testimony to show others that he is real.

I dedicate this book to everyone who believed in me, even when I wanted to give up, and I didn't believe in myself.

To my mother Jessie Thomas, who I love and miss dearly, who tought me, many life lessons and they began with praying. Without her there would be no me.

To all the characters in this book, each one of them has played a very intricate part in my book my life as well as my journey. My experience through this journey allowed me to see there was something vital that I need to share. I thank everyone who played a part in my life even the not so good. This has made me a stronger woman.

ACKNOWLEDGEMENTS

My inspiration for this book started when I came to a realization on how so many people are just stuck in this life's journey. I realized I can help people become aware in what they are thinking, be free from fear, and to live without limits after sharing a very heartfelt discussion with one of my dear friends, Kimberly Lloyd. The discussion revolved around one thing: how I am able to help other people and show them how the thoughts that they think shape their entire lives and how to become more vigilant in the thoughts that they think.

INTRODUCTION

The book, *Illusion Versus Reality*, was written and created by author Ruby Larry. This book was written in hopes of helping people deal with difficult life changes and situations, and to help people become more aware and conscious in their thinking. Throughout the book, you will see problems, as well as solutions to those problems that we may all face in our daily lives. You will notice people who will try shortcuts to make it through life. But because they are trapped in the illusion, they are unaware that they are in an illusion – they ultimately begin to realize that there are no shortcuts.

CHAPTER 1: WASTING TIME

Today I decided to come to the park and write. I had something on my mind on August 19; I will be one year older than what I am today. What a wonderful blessing and a gift of life from God. I am at the point in my life where I want to build something, like a husband and a family; a life. I have dated a few men in my past and it ended up nowhere. What a waste of time. I came to the realization that if you don't want to build a life with me, then you must be here to tear mine down or distract me and keep me off track, wasting time. Time is one of your most valuable assets, so why waste something so valuable?

I had dated this wonderful man in the past, very good looking, nice; it was everything I was looking for. I saw this man for about two years or more, and I wanted to know what his plans were. He really could not tell me, and to me that indicated that he did not have any. I knew then it was time to move on because if you don't want a good woman and a life, then you must want a bad one. I wanted more than that hell! I deserve more. I am a wonderful person, beautiful, I am happy, good career, good cook, and a clean house. I thought that's what men were looking for. Yes! Men. I think he has a lot of growing up to do. You've heard the saying, "What you want might make you cry and what you need might pass you by if you don't catch it." If I want to build something, I need a solid foundation for my building to stand on. You cannot build a castle in the sky—what will it stand on? I guarantee it will fall. Sometimes your foundation can fall too, if you do not build it strong enough. So, if you do not want to build a life with me, then what are you here for? To tear down what I am trying to build is the only conclusion I can see, or use what I have. I guess some people grow up faster than others. When you do not have your things together, it is hard to build. Some people waste so much time doing the wrong things in life that if or when they do find someone worth building with, they have wasted their most valuable time doing so much wrong. Instead of what is right, they do not have anything at the end. If you do not have your things together, what can you offer me (or vice versa)? Nothing but sex—

you can get that anywhere. Who want just that? I think I deserve more than that. Who wants what they can get anywhere?

Dear reader, lovers come and go. I learned that you have to make a man buy it, and when I say buy it, I mean a marriage because you respect what you pay for, and if they do not buy it, then you get no respect. So when the man you're dealing with says that he loves you, make him prove it. If you do not, then he is only going to play with you. So it is time to move around because you will waste one of your most valuable assets: your time. Who has something so valuable to waste? Not me.

If I want to build something, I must first have a plan, just like I am a hairstylist, and if I want to open a day spa in my near future, and when the builders come to check out the area where I am going to build my day spa, they're going to need to see a floor plan. So say, for instance, that I'm the builder in my own life, as for each individual. If I don't have a plan for my life, how can I build anything? When I asked the man that I had been dating, "What are your plans?" he could not tell me anything except, "I have dreams, I have goals." And I said, "Well…what are they? If you cannot articulate them to me, then apparently you do not have any." So it was time for me to move because he would have continued wasting one of my most valuable assets, my time.

You know, I see a lot of people doing whatever, not busy building, and I am like, wow! Just wasting their life doing nothing, not having anything. I see a lot of people who think they are living. They try to sell drugs, they steal, they do whatever they can do to make money, but they never really grow. They end back at square one with even more problems. By then I figure you have had some kind of encounter with the police, then are sent to jail, and the life you should have been building is put on hold because you have to pay your debt to society. On top of that, you are now a felon—what a disaster. If you want it to turn out right, then you must follow the right instructions. I like to use this as an illustration. If I want to bake a cake, I will see that the instructions say to put three eggs in the cake mix. But if I do what I want to do as opposed to what the instructions are telling me, how do you think the cake is going to turn out? Likewise with your life—if you do not do the right things, and instead you do what you want, how you want, then the result will turn out not like you expected it to. You should follow directions. I hear a lot of people say "I love you." But how many really know what love is? Now you will never know what love is until you lose it, and then you will know that it was everything you were looking for. What I am trying to say is, never take anything for granted and assume that it will always be there because just when you think it will, it will be gone. If you love me, then show me because the truth is generally seen and rarely is it heard. If you cannot show and prove your love, then you are a waste of my most valuable asset, my time.

Sometimes we do not recognize our dreams inside reality. We are unaware of exactly what is real. We walk around daydreaming. Sometimes I think it's good to lose something, that way you work hard to get it back. And when you do, you will take care of it a little better. Loss makes you appreciate it more, makes you cherish it more and not take it for granted. I have learned that life is a series of decisions that will ultimately lead you to or away from your destiny or ultimate destination. You have to make a choice if you want something good or bad, because you only have one of two choices, and you need to be aware of your choices and make a conscious decision. If you do not, then one will be chosen for you. I want something good in my life. Like I said, if you don't want something good, then you must be looking for something bad. I guess it is all the things that you don't want, to lead you to the things you do want.

Here is another one of my illustrations: I go shopping at the mall, and I tell one of my friends that I am with to hold on while I go into a store; I know exactly what I want and I will not be long. So I get what I want, pay for it, then I am on my way. If you don't know what you want when you go in the store, then you may pick up anything—the wrong thing or something you really did not want. You must know what you want and choose to make a conscious decision or one will be chosen for you. If you don't make a conscious decision to choose good, then unconsciously you will choose something bad.

You know what really amazes me is that people want something different, but they continue to do the same thing. If you don't follow your instructions, like I mentioned earlier, then you will continue to get the same results. That is the definition of insanity: to keep doing the same thing and expect it to turn out differently. I was right when I said it was time to move on because the man I was dating did not have a plan. If you don't have a plan or know where you are going, then you will end up anywhere.

People are always trying to read the motives behind your actions. Another thing I have learned is that when you do the right thing but for the wrong reason, you will soon stop. I guess change comes eventually; after winter must come spring. In order to change anything in your life, you must get your mind set on what you want so it can then grow up in your life. I think one of the biggest changes a person can do is change some of the company you keep. You need to watch the kind of people you deal with, because people who are not on the right track can get you off of your track and keep you from accomplishing what you were set out to do. When you get off track, it can take your time. To me it seems like we are racing against time, when time is really an illusion that doesn't exist. It is something we came up with to keep track of things. So if time is an illusion that doesn't exist, then you really have no time to waste. I hear a lot of women say what they want in a man, what are you willing to bring to the table? You can't get something you are not. In life I learned that you don't get what you want, you get exactly what you are. Whatever you give is just what you get. If you are not going to do good, then you should not expect good.

I like to look at life like riding a bike: to stay on a bike you have to keep peddling, to keep moving. I used to hear my cousin say "a mind is a terrible thing to waste." I never really understood what he was talking about because I was so young, but now I know. I thank God for granting me the serenity to accept the things I cannot change, the courage to change the things that I can, and the wisdom to know the difference.

CHAPTER 2: ILLUSION VERSUS REALITY

Today I went to the swimming pool to meet a friend of mine named Ashley. I wanted to tell her I was thinking about writing a book. She thought it was a great idea. She also started to talk about some guy name Dupree that she had been dating for about three years. The guy she is dealing with doesn't want a serious relationship, and she know he doesn't, but she continues to see him anyway. I asked her, "Why do you waste your time?" I told her, "If you don't stand for something, you will fall for anything." Change comes eventually. Have you ever heard the story about the dog sitting on the nail? Well... there was a man sitting on the porch with his dog, and another man walked by and said, "Why is that dog sitting on that nail? He keeps moaning." The man on the porch said, "I guess it doesn't hurt badly enough, so when it hurts badly enough, he will move." You see, you can never change anyone. The only person you can change is you.

People tend to do what they want until they get tired. I just woke up this morning I watched a little Creflo Dollar Ministries on television. Then Edward Young, another minister, came on. His message really touched me—it was about betrayal. It is always the person you love the most that does you that cruel, harsh, cold, the kind of betrayal that knocks you to your knees where it feels like someone has handed you your heart. We have all been at this point one time or another. I just went through this same kind of betrayal—some kind of way I pulled through, or as some people say, I broke through. I thank God because if I hadn't gone through that, I would not be who I am today. I see it as the overcoming of a thing that you can see increase in your life, or in other words, God is preparing me for what he has for me. You know what they say, no pain no gain—if it doesn't hurt, then you cannot have it. Nothing worthwhile comes easily. In order to get something, you got to go through something. Life to me is like a mirror, a mirror is a reflection of what you think. In Proverbs 23:7, the Bible says, so does a man think it in his heart or soul, so is he. Or so he lives it.

Yesterday, I was riding with my Cousin Troy. He and his girlfriend and a bunch of his friends had been hanging out and partying all night. He was complaining about his girlfriend, she had scratched him up because they had gotten into a fight. I asked him, "Do you like your girlfriend?" He said, "I love her." I asked, "So…when are you getting married?" He said, "I don't have any money, I don't want a stressed out marriage." Do you get the picture? If you don't have your things together, then you cannot build anything. When you are too focused on doing the wrong things, you never get anything out of it. It gives you the illusion that there is something there, but in reality, you have nothing. Instead of hanging out Troy could have been working on getting his life together, Those are the types of activities that keep you off track of what you should be doing, like getting yourself together so you can have money. After the sex, partying, and hanging out with his friends, what did he gain? Nothing but sex. What is that? Nothing. Remember, you can get that anywhere. You hear a lot of people say, "Ahhhhh, it's just sex," and I think to myself that if it is nothing, then why waste your time doing nothing—as for me I would rather be doing something.

My phone rings and it is a friend I know named Darryl. Darryl is going through a divorce. He knew that during his marriage he had done some things wrong, and he knew that one day he would have to pay for his wrong doings. He told me, "I did not know that it would hurt like this." Although this is a concept that we all understand, we don't think that this will happen to us. What goes around, comes around. Let me explain why it works like this. Your life is a mirror of what you think, the mirror reflects reality. Because you are the one who is doing the thinking, you are the one who gets the reflection. So you see, you can never harm anyone with your thoughts. It is almost like a boomerang—whatever you put out, that's what you want back, so whatever you do, that's what you want done to you. As for Darryl, his wife has moved on, she has left him alone and empty. When he was out cheating on his wife, he had the illusion that he was going to get something better than what he had. In reality, he had nothing. The mirror reflects reality, but it is also a perfect tool for deception. Because he was going to get nothing, in reality he had nothing. Whatever he was looking for, he already had. All he did was waste time to get nothing.

Today I called Ashley, I wanted to know what she had been up to. It sounded like she had just woken up. She and I started to talk about men and why some of them don't have things in order, and why it takes them so long to grow up. She started to tell me about one of her friends name Breanne and how she met this man and after one year they were married. Come to find out the man was fresh out of prison and had been lying about his real identity. She knew she wanted a man, but she didn't know what kind of man she was looking for. Just like the illustration I gave earlier about going to the mall, if you don't know what you want when you go into the store, then you may end up picking up anything, something you really didn't want. So that's why you must be aware of your choices, make a conscious decision or unconsciously you will choose badly. In reality, Breanne gained nothing—she has lost a lot of her time; who has something so valuable to waste?

Today I was thinking about myself and how I made it to where I am. I worked at this strip club called The 20s Show Girl. When I first started, I needed extra money to take off a financial strain after getting out of an ugly break up. At the time, I was working at this marketing company, and I was really tired of that job. It seemed like I couldn't make ends meet, and on top of that, I hated the job, so I quit and continued to dance. I was making lots of money—I would spend some and save some. I always thought it was wise to save a little. I met many different kinds of people in this business; you got the girls who work just for drugs, sex, money, you name it. I knew this was not a place I would like to be, not for a long time anyway. So I decided to go to school to become an EMT, emergency medical technician. I really learned a lot of good stuff, but I really hated it. I see where I wasted some time and never gained anything out of it because I didn't use the EMT school for anything. So I stopped and started going to another college for cosmetology. I have always had a passion for making people look better. When you look good, you feel good. So I went to school and continued to work at The 20s Show Girl. After a while, I stopped working at The 20s Show Girl. They wanted me to work too many days, and I needed the free time to go to school and study. So I started working at another strip club called Lipstix. It was a little different because it was new, and I liked the idea of working a couple nights a week while able to still go to school full time. While I worked at this club, I met a lot of nice people, lots of nice girls, and it really surprised me how many girls had been working there for so long. Not that I was any better than they were, but I had a plan. My plan was to make money to live and continue to go to school in the process. Unless you have a strong mind, I would never recommend that anyone do this kind of job. The money seems so great, so you continue to do this—it is so easy, but it really has a way to trap you.

I knew this lady that worked there by the name of Goldie. She and I became somewhat cool—we would hang out, outside of the club, go on vacation. We even went to church together a couple of times. Whenever she would drink, she would turn into a different person. I would say you shouldn't drink if it makes you act like that! She is quick to say, "You don't tell me how to act, I been here 17 years." She would say it as if she had a degree in nursing, like she was proud. I, on the other hand, would never tell anybody that I was working at a strip club for 17 years and have nothing to show for it. You get the illusion that you are gaining something, but in reality, you have nothing. All she has done is waste a bunch of time to gain nothing. As for me I am still working on that day spa.

Ring! It's 6:00 a.m. Hello! It is my uncle's girlfriend, Liyah. She is upset because she and my Uncle Charlie got into an argument that escalated to a fight. Charlie is now in jail for domestic violence, and Liyah has to handle everything on her own now. She has to get a job to pay the bills. She never went to school, so she has no education, and on top of that, when she met Charlie, he had a wife. I say that Liyah was one of those types of people to come into Charlie's life to keep him off track of what he should be doing. Because he was distracted, his decision changed his destination. So he went to build elsewhere with no foundation for the building to stand on. Liyah always wondered why they argued and fought so much; they called each other everything but a child of God. Like the recipe, you left out the eggs—you started off wrong. Do you get it? You cannot get right when you start off wrong from the beginning.

Last night I spoke to a friend of mine named Steve. He is in the process of trying to buy a house—he complains about how he wants to get out of his mother's house. He always says, "What do I look like? 40 years old, and I still live with my mother." When he was young, he went to prison for drugs. When you are too busy doing the wrong things, you never get anything out of it. If you are not going to do good, then don't expect good.

I remember when I was about 23 or 24 years old. At that point I thought I was grown, you could not tell me anything, I thought I knew it all. I had a boyfriend named Alex, and when we first met, everything seem good, so we later got a house together. He became abusive, both verbally and physically. The abuse got worse, so bad that the police were involved. I was the type of young woman who has always been independent; he was the type of man who wanted full power and control over everything. He would try to tear me down by saying things like, "You're never going to be anything; all you have is a nice body." I thought I wanted a man, but I didn't know what kind of man I wanted so I picked up anything—the wrong thing, something I really didn't want, I now see what I really want is a good man because I am a good woman. You do good, you can expect good. My good man has not arrived yet, but I know he will be showing up soon. Sometimes blindness finds us and leads us into ignorance and we become lifeless. These are the type of people who try to take the easy way out. They want things but they don't want to work to get them. They choose to take the easy way out doing all the wrong things, and they have an illusion that they are gaining. The illusion is really a mirror, but it is a deceiver's mirror—in reality, they have nothing, they lost everything. It is almost like they are chasing something that is really not there. When you do this you waste a lot of your time doing nothing. Sometimes when you lose, you win, and when you win, you lose.

The mailman is at the door. I received a letter from Maurice; Maurice is a man that I used to date years ago. He has been in prison for about 15 years. In his letter, he talked about my cousin, Dana; he wanted to know why Dana was spreading rumors about him, and slandering everyone's name, including mine. I told Maurice when we spoke on the phone that I really didn't care what Dana has to say about me, at least I will not be lost in oblivion and forgotten about. Dana had a rough childhood growing up—her mother abused her, and she never knew her father that well. She started using drugs and has lost her children. Because she likes to use drugs, she cannot get her children back. She will not do the hard work needed to get them back like getting a job, rehabilitating, and parenting, whatever it takes. She also never finished school, so she has no education. Because she chooses to smoke and use drugs, not do the right thing, her decision changed her destination. Her reality is blurred or she is blind. She has the illusion that she is gaining something, but she is being deceived—she has lost everything, including her children. In reality, she has nothing, except wasted time to gain nothing. As for Maurice, he thought he was gaining something too; in reality, he lost a lot of his life in prison. When you do the wrong things, you never gain anything out of it.

Okay, back to me. Remember the guy I was dating? You know, the one who didn't have a plan? He and I lived in two different states, and I was willing to move to where he was since I didn't have any baggage. I am a professional hairstylist, so a job would be nothing for me to find. I told him, "I don't know how long this long distance thing is going to work for me. I am ready to move forward—it can be with you, if you choose, or it is going to be with someone else. I would marry you and your three kids if I thought that's what you wanted. What do you want?" He said, "I am going through a lot right now, I will call you in due time. I will come to you in person." That sounded believable, but it made no sense, and when something doesn't make sense, it is usually not true. So I gave him time to get back to me, but he never called.

When I tried to call him, he would ignore my phone calls. I grew very angry because he wouldn't respond. My heart was torn. It was a dense, crushing, geophysical force, a bend to the core type of feeling. Almost like the wind had been knocked out of me, kind of like I was gasping for breath. He thought if he ignores me, that I would come to see him—that's what he was used to. He was used to a woman surrendering to him so he could have his way.

I thought about it for a minute. I said to myself, "I may have unsettled him, and when you do that and make the other person play by your rules, they want to hurt you." I knew this was some kind of a set up for me to come to him and see him with another woman, knowing I loved him the way I did. I thought, "Why am I the one chasing and not directing the show? He is the one who wouldn't answer the phone. Plus, he lives in another state. If I wanted to see him, I would have to come to him." What I did instead was mail his clothes back to him that he had left at my place. I used a Dallas address to made it look like I had moved out of state, and I never called him again. He had something in his mind to do to me to hurt me, and all I wanted to do was love him. My grandfather use to say, "While you're digging one hole for someone else, make sure you dig two because you don't know who might fall in it first." Mailing his clothes back with the out-of-state return address and never calling him again lowered his resistance. Now I get so many restricted phone calls, but I don't want to be bothered with him. He has been hit with the mirror. What goes around, comes around. He was thinking of doing something to harm me—those were his thoughts, so he got the reflection. My grandfather was right—the hole he planned for me, he fell in it instead, and the funny part about it was that he didn't know that I knew it is him calling. Now he is wondering what I am doing and who I am with, and if he wants to know, he has to come see. But he doesn't know what to expect. That's how I felt, and that is a horrible feeling. Well, I guess he will get over it in due time. As for me, my mind is at ease. A friend of my grandmother used to say, "The only time your conscious bothers you is when you have done something wrong—that's the only judge and juror you're ever going to need in life." I guess he feels he was wrong because he is still wondering. He had the illusion that whatever he was doing, he was winning, but in reality, I am gone. Sometimes when you think you win, you really lose, and when you lose, you really win. Good always comes out on top. I got the last laugh.

My phone rings. It's Lynn, one of my childhood friends. I looked at the phone and thought to myself, "I wonder what she wants." She is so crazy, I mean literally. When we were younger, she never acted like she does now. I think men and bad relationships drove her crazy over the years. I have known her for 20 years or more, and I never remember her acting weird like she does. Besides that, I was cleaning when she called, so I said to myself, "Hmmmmm, I think I will call her back later. After I finished cleaning, I called her back.

She said, "I was calling to tell you my brother is in town."

I said, "Who? Kelly?"

She said, "No, TJ. He came to town to put a tombstone on Mom's gravesite."

I said, "That was nice and thoughtful."

She said, "He's mad because no one came to see him when he was in jail."

Well…he made his own choices in life that led him to jail—it is his fault. For every choice you make, there is a consequence.

Then she said, "What happened to the guy you where dating?"

I said, "Girrrl, I left that alone because he didn't have any plans for his life and I do. I think it is best to move forward and never look back unless that's where you plan to be. If I continued to do the same thing and expect a different result, that is crazy! If he wants to move forward and try something different, then I may consider it. I want someone who I can build a life with, someone who wants what I want."

Knock, knock! "Who is it?"

"It's Janise."

"What's going on?"

"Girl, I caught my husband cheating on me.

"What! What happened?"

"Well… he came home from work, a cell phone fell out of his jacket and hit the floor. First of all, he didn't have a cell phone, or at least I didn't know he had one. When it fell, I kind of kicked it under the couch, and when he left, I went through it. I got all the numbers off of it. When he got home, I asked him, 'Orlando, where did you get that cell phone?' He said he found it, I knew he was lying because I saw the charger plugged into the wall, but I never mentioned anything about the charger to him before. I later called the number back on the cell phone, one particular number stood out from the rest because it had been dialed more than the others, so that is the one I called back. When I called, a lady answered. I hung up, and she called back. The phone rang. 'Hello!' 'Did someone call me?' I said, 'Who is this?' She said, 'This is raven.' I said, 'Do you know Jordan?' I mentioned the kids' names first. She said, 'No!' I said, 'Do you know Mickey?' She said, 'No!' I said, 'Well... do you know Orlando?' She said, 'Yes!' I said, 'How do you know him?' She said, 'We're friends.' I said, 'This is his wife, hold on, let me get him for you. Orlando! Telephone! Raven wants to speak to you!' Girl, you should have seen the look on his face—that told it all, his eyes looked like he had seen a ghost. Later that day I called the number back to speak with Raven. I told her, 'I am not calling to start any trouble, but are you sleeping with my husband?' She said, 'Yes.' I was devastated.

I asked her how long she had been seeing him. She said, 'For two months or more.' I said, 'Thank you! And I will not bother you again.' When he made it back home I told him that I was aware of his creeping. I told him what I knew, and I kicked him out. He moved back to Ohio, and now he continues to call and try to apologize, but I really can't trust him anymore. How do I know he will not try this again?"

I said, "You really don't know. You been with him for 12 years. Are you sure you want to give it all up? Nobody's perfect."

"Yeah, I know, but I, I just don't know," she said.

"Well, you know what's good for you or not," I said.

She said, "I am so mad I wasted 12 years of my life for nothing."

Orlando thought he was winning, but cheaters never win. It gives you the illusion that you are winning, but in reality, he lost everything, including his wife and children. Now he has to start over—what a waste of time. Just as I mentioned earlier, if God has already given Orlando someone to build a life with, then what is Raven doing in the picture? If you are not helping me build, then you must be here to tear it down. Orlando was being deceived that what he was getting was better than what he already had. And in the end, he gained nothing—he traded good for something bad, and he wasted a bunch of time to get nothing. As for Orlando, he is currently in Ohio, and Janise wants a divorce. Maybe God will send her something better to build with.

CHAPTER 3: DECISION MAKING, DETERMINE YOUR DESTINATION

I spoke to my sister Denise today. I wanted to wish her a happy birthday. She started to talk about one of her good friends named Angela. Angela was over to Monique's house. Monique and my cousin Dana are sisters. Dana asked Angela, "When have you talked to Denise?" Angela said that she was kind of passive because she knew that Dana and Denise had gotten into a fight. Dana and Denise used to be the best of cousins until they had a falling out about Dana's husband—Dana thinks her husband slept with Denise, but she can't prove it. Years ago, Dana and Denise both used to be on drugs, and they both lost their children. Denise did all the hard work to get her children back, but Dana, on the other hand, has not gotten her children back yet. To be honest, I don't think she wants them back.

About a month ago, Denise came into town, and we had to attend a funeral. One of our close cousins, Edward, was murdered in cold blood. When Denise got into town, Dana came by to hang out, but Dana had cruel intentions from the start. She was bitter about the thought that Denise had slept with her husband, and her life didn't turn out quite the way she wanted it to. Dana still uses drugs, and she tried to get Denise to start using again too. Denise knows she has been down this road before and knew how hard it was to go the right way. Remember, you need to watch the kind of people you deal with, because people who aren't on the right track can get you off track, and before you know it, you will end up someplace you didn't intend to be. It may seem appealing first— the deception will always look appealing so it can get you to go in that direction. It makes you seem like you are getting something, but in reality, you lose. Denise chose a different route, and her decision changed her destination. Life is a series of decision making that leads you to or away from your destiny or destination. As for Dana, she is still being deceived. She thinks she is getting something, but in reality, she has nothing. Your mindset will determine your life-set, so if you don't change your mind, then nothing in your life will change because we can only do what we think about. Our body doesn't operate on its own—it does what it is told to do.

In Romans 12:2, it says, "Be not conformed to this world: but be transformed by the renewal of your mind," But we have to ask ourselves this question: who, or what, is setting your mind? Where did you get that way of thinking? Whether you are saved or not, the devil is after your mind so he can keep you blind to what God said we can have. So either it will be God or it will be the devil, and it's up to us to choose whether we win or lose. And, dear readers, I choose to win.

Steve called me tonight and said he was close to getting his house. Everything was working out good because he is doing good, and when you do good, then you can expect good. He talked about a bar in Indianapolis called The Frosty Mug. He had read on the internet at work that the people who owned this bar were selling drugs, and the elder people who lived across the street started to wonder why the people who went inside the bar wouldn't be inside very long. They grew suspicious and someone called the police. The police raided the bar and everyone involved went to jail. The owner of this business was deceived. He had the illusion that he was gaining something, but the reality was that he lost everything. He lost his place of business and his freedom. I don't know if he had a family or not, but if he did, he probably lost them too. When you are too busy doing the wrong things, you never gain anything. All you do is waste your time to gain nothing. Remember, the deception is always going to look appealing so it can get you to go that way. People need to come to the realization that if you don't do right, then you are not going to get it or have anything. If you do get anything, you will never be happy, and it will not last long. When you figure out the fundamental principal of what kind of harvest you want to reap, then you will not waste your time doing anything harmful.

CHAPTER 4: THE MIRROR AND REALITY

Give and it shall be given. This is the ultimate secret of the universe. Why? Because everything flows as exchange of energy from one place to another. The other day I was watching the movie *The Color Purple,* and when Sealy was getting ready to leave with Shug Avery, and Mister. Was trying to keep Sealy from leaving with Shug. I think Sealy was going to move up to Memphis with Shug and Shug's husband. Mister grabbed her arm like he was going to pull her out of the car, and Sealy pulled back and told him, "Until you do right by me, anything you think about is going to fail." I guess Sealy understood that if you aren't going to do right, then everything you try to do without doing it right will fail. You never get far. She later told him, "Everything you done to me, I already done to you." I can see here where she understood the mirror. Remember, when it is your thoughts doing the thinking, bad or good, then because they are your thoughts, you are the one who gets the reflection. Your life is a mirror or a reflection of what you think. If you can understand this concept, then you will watch what you think, do, and say. The Bible clearly tells us that so does a man think it in his heart, so is he.

I stopped by my Uncle Charlie's today to see his girlfriend, and my cousin Darren was over there. Darren is Edward's brother, and Edward is the one who was recently murdered. Darren was still mourning really badly. He had been hearing rumors about who killed his brother, and he wanted to go and get some kind of a revenge on them. He and I were riding together one day, and he asked, "What do you think I should do?" I told him, "By you doing that, you can't bring him back." Darren is not aware of the fundamental principles of the universe. In Roman 12:19, it says, "Dearly beloved, avenge not yourselves, but rather give place unto wrath; for it is written, vengeance is mine; I will repay saith the Lord."

I said, "It will surface, you will soon know who did this."

When I walked in the door of my Uncle Charlie's house, Darren said, "You know the guy who killed Edward has been shot.

He is in the hospital on life support. Someone shot him in the head."

I said, "How do you know he is the one who did it?"

He said, "Do you remember Tonya, the ex-girlfriend I used to date?"

I said, "Yes!"

"She hangs out in the 40th Street neighborhood. Her friend Kim that was dating one of the guys that hangs out in the same neighborhood overheard them bragging about it, and she told Tonya, my ex-girlfriend, and Tonya told me."

I said, "Remember what I said? I told you, you don't have to do anything. What goes around comes around."

The guy who killed Edward had thoughts of death and killing, and because it was his thoughts, he was the one who got the reflection. You can never harm anyone with what you think. Remember, your life is a mirror of what you think. When you come to understand this, you will watch what you think, because what you think about, you bring about. There is no greater mystery than this. We keep seeking reality when, in fact, we are reality. Sometimes we can't see for looking. Here's another way of saying this: look, it's right in front of your eyes. When people are unconscious, or daydreaming, not aware of exactly what is real, they fail to see things how they really are. They need to wake up and see the light or the truth. In order to understand, we must remain in the darkness of not knowing. That way you will come to see the truth or the light on your own. Once you become enlighten, you will see through the illusion of life and will know what reality really is. Physical reality is an illusion that's created by consciousness or conscious thinking. When you do unconscious thinking, you live the life of an illusion that is not true, and when reality hits you or the light comes on, you see the real truth.

This morning I was watching the news which was talking about some little girl who was kidnapped when she was 11 years old. A sex offender had taken her and held her captive for 18 years, and when they found her, she was still alive—she was 29 years old. The man who kidnapped her was thinking thoughts of captivity, and now he is held captive by the police. When you do bad things you never gain anything out of it. You get the illusion that you are getting something, but in reality you have lost. When people come to the realization that you can't do anything bad and get away with it, they will stop wasting time for nothing.

On the movie *Menace to Society* there was a guy named Cane who lived a hardcore life of robbing, drugs, and guns. Cane once said that his grandfather asked him if he cares whether he lives or dies. He said he didn't know. I can see here where he didn't make a conscious decision of what he wanted. He got shot in a drive-by shooting, and his life started to flash before his eyes. You could hear him narrate his story. He said at the end that it all catches up with you, and now he wanted to live, but it was too late. Your mind or your thoughts are reality, and reality or your thoughts are your mind. Awareness is power because awareness gives you a choice. Choice is an illusion created by those in control for those who are not to be in control. You must know the principals of the universe and how everything works. You need awareness so you can make a conscious decision. If you don't, then one will be chosen for you. Remember, you only have one of two choices—each step of your way you must always choose between the two. The ending of one choice is always the beginning of the other. Choose well—your future is entirely in your hands.

These benefits are available to everyone; they are withheld from no one. A good decision leads to a life of success and good fortune. A bad decision leads to a lesson of hardship and despair, only so you will ultimately come to know the truth. Truth seems paradoxal only when your mind is cluttered with untruth. Each choice is always in front of you, both good and bad. So choose wisely. Good seems to be the only way to go. Why would you choose anything else?

Ashley called me today, but I missed her phone call. She left a message that said, "This is Ashley, call me, I want to talk to you."

I called her back, and she said, "What are you doing going over to Dupree's house?"

I said, "What! What are you talking about?"

She said, "I saw your car parked by his house over on Pinkney Street. I called your phone and you didn't answer it. I called Dupree's phone and he didn't answer his phone either. I thought you were my friend. How could you do this to me?"

I told her, "First of all, I didn't know Dupree lived on Pinckney Street. Second, I was over at my aunt's house that lives on Pinkney Street."

She later apologized saying, "I am sorry; I thought you were trying to see him behind my back. I see I keep making a fool out of myself. Well, I am going to work. I will call you later."

I can see here where she has the illusion that this man is hers, and that I was over to his house behind her back. The illusion is always designed to fool you into thinking it is something else. The reality is that man is single although they recently dated; she is under the impression that this man is hers. He can do as he pleases; besides I was over at my aunt's house anyway. Remember, the illusion is always going to trick you into thinking that it is something other than it really is. I guess the mind always need room to wonder—when a person already knows what to expect, they have nothing to wonder about. That's when reality has hit you, when you come to know the truth.

CHAPTER 5: TRUTH IS REALITY

Let's talk about truth. Truth is good because it gives you awareness that you need to make a conscious decision. When you lie to someone, it's like you don't give them a choice to decide, and that is so unfair. What if God, the creator of all things, did not tell us the truth? Take your time and think about that for a minute. God is genuine, for he is straightforward. He has nothing to hide, so there is nothing to defend. Untruth is a form of betrayal; betrayal is like you have been pushed into a pit.

I had a discussion with my Uncle Charlie about truth and fact. He said, "No! They are the same thing." I said, "No! They are not!" The truth is the actual state of matter, conformity with facts, and a fact is something that has been known to happen, but it always needs proof. And it is subject to change. As for the truth, it doesn't need proof—either it is or it isn't. It's hard for scientists to make up seas, make up trees, so why do we turn our backs on the truth? I sometimes wonder why people don't tell the truth. I guess, at the end, it all catches up with you. To me it seems or appears that our universe is designed to work a certain way—there are principals to operate within it and by the time some people figure that out, it is too late for them to live. That's how it will be when you die and your soul leaves your body. Because you didn't make a conscious decision to do what God told you to do when you were in your physical body, then once you leave your physical body, you lose the right to decide. And so a choice will be made for you. By the time you realize that you want to live, it will be too late. You know, we were never created to die, but because of the decisions that were made in that garden, that changed the destination. But God knew we had no way to save ourselves, and He wanted us to have a good life, so He sent Jesus so that through him, we will be saved. He let us be a free moral agent to choose what path we wanted. We were taken out of eternity and put into time to see what we would do with time.

He says in Deuteronomy 30:19, "I call heaven and earth to record this day against you. I place before you a life and death, a blessing and a cursing: therefore choose life,

So you and your seed may live: We know a blessing is an empowerment to prosper where, on the other hand, a curse is an empowerment to fail, and it's up to us to choose whether we win or lose. And this is true. Have you noticed anyone that tries to do anything without doing it the right way? It does not work—it is designed to work only one way, and they keep doing it and doing it and they continue to get the same results. If you did what you always did, then you get what you always got. You have to follow the instruction that God the great creator of all things left us. His words are truth and when you continue in His word, then you are His disciples indeed. Then you shall know the truth, and the truth shall set you free. So it's when you continue to do His word then you will be free. The key word here is "continue." How do you know what God has said if you don't read your instruction manual? I feel some people want to accept deception instead of what is true. These kinds of people live a lie. Like I mentioned earlier, the best way to come to know the truth is to remain in the darkness of not knowing, that way you will come to know the truth on your own.

When we see a nice car, we acknowledge its creator. When we see a nice pair of shoes, we acknowledge who designed them. When we see the universe, part of it is visible to us—how can we fail to acknowledge its creator? And when you buy a new car, it comes with an owner's manual on how to operate it. When you buy shoes, they come with instructions on how to care for your shoes. So likewise with your life—you need to follow your instructions, this is the truth.

My Uncle Charlie called me today from jail. He wanted me to give his attorney a call to see if she could get him into court. He was trying to get out of jail; he had accepted a plea bargain with the court so he could get out of jail. I was unable to get a hold of his attorney, so he has to stay in jail until he go to trial. Liyah put a protection order on him—the court system told her that's what she had to do because there are children involved. If the police have to come out again due to the domestic dispute, then her children will be taken and placed in a foster home.

Janise came to pick me up we are going to a 2008 , change convention to see Dr. Creflo dollar his message was about fear he read a scripture from 2nd timothy 1-7 God has not given us the spirit of fear; but of power, and of love, and of a sound mind. If you have fear, then you know it was not from God. He said the devil uses fear to gain access into your life, because when you fear, you make all of your decisions based on that fear. Then he talked about how people let fear keep them from doing things in life because they are afraid. He later said that when you find yourself afraid, then you must be in disbelief. Fear and unbelief go hand in hand—whenever you are in fear, you need to ask yourself what it is that you don't believe. The truth is, God will do whatever he said he would do. In order for this to work, you must believe it. If you don't believe it, then it will not work for you. In Job 3:25 says, "The thing I feared the most has come up on me, and which I was afraid of is come unto me. Whatever you have the potential to think—faith or fear—then that's what your reality will be. Remember, because you are the one doing the thinking, then you are the one who gets the reflection.

Denise called me today. She and I talked about why she and Dana were fighting. She told me that it was because some stuff had happened a long time ago when they both where on drugs. She told me she did sleep with Dana's husband, and she had apologized to Dana and thought everything was okay.

Denise continued telling me the story. She said, "I didn't know that she was still bitter about that. When she came to pick me up after I made it into town, we were riding around drinking some Hennessey. Dana's husband went inside the store to get a pack of cigarettes, and she got mad because she thought that he bought the cigarettes for me. She started saying little things like, 'I been with him all day and he didn't get me any cigarettes.' It never occurred to me that she was directing that statement to me. As time went on as we were riding in her husband's van, out of nowhere she just hit me so hard in my face I saw stars. I kicked her into the windshield, almost causing her husband have an accident. Then she kicked me out of the van in the middle of the night at like 3:30 a.m. Remember, I am from out of town and it has been a minute since I had been there, so I really didn't know where I was. I had to walk to find a taxi station to catch a ride back to Aunt Valencia's house."

When my sister told me this, I went to look for Dana, but she was nowhere to be found. I was going to ask her why she hit my sister in the face, but I came to learn that she had taken off because she stole $4,000 from her husband. When she took the money, she had cut a hole in his pants pocket while he was asleep. She ran off and went to hide out and no one knows where she is. I can see here why Dana can't understand why things are not working out too good for her. If you're not going to do good, then don't expect good.

I ran into my ex, Alex today. I always try to say hello to him, I don't want to seem bitter. For some reason, I think he is very angry because of the break up. After we split up, he went buck wild, sleeping with all kinds of different women. Now he has a lot of children, all by different women. One time I went to his sister's house for the holiday (she always invited me over for the holiday), and she said to me, "To tell you the truth, Alex has not been the same since you two split up." When Alex put his hands on me, I had to leave because it seemed to get worse. I told him that it was the last time he will ever put his hands on me or any other woman for that matter. I called the police, and they took him to jail. When he was in jail, I called a moving company and had them move everything out of the house. When Alex got out of jail, everything was gone including me, and I didn't speak to him for about three or four years after that. He was very angry with me, and for some reason, he acts like he is not angry, but the reality shows something totally different. I remember that he always said he wanted some kids, so he got just what he wanted. He didn't have them with me like he thought he was going to, but he did get some. I guess he didn't make a conscious decision. He was not exact on what he wanted. You must know what you want, or you will get anything.

CHAPTER 6: ILLUSION CREATES YOUR REALITY

Darryl called me and is kind of upset because of the decision he made to cheat on his wife. He has the blues; now he is lonely. I tried to comfort him, but nothing can seem to fill that empty void. He didn't realize what he had until it was gone, and now he sees that it was everything that he was looking for all along. He had taken her for granted and assumed that she would always be there.

Ring! "Hello?"

"It's Lynn, hey! I just called to tell you that I am having a little girl."

"Congratulations! What will you call her?"

"Todd wants me to name her Paris."

"That's a cute name for a little girl. What about Elena?"

She said, "That is pretty too. I want you to come and see me today."

"What's wrong with your car?" I asked her.

"I had to pawn it to pay my rent."

I said, "Lynn, if that man you are with can't help you, then what do you need him for?"

"He helps me! The other day he took me to get a wig."

I just shook my head in disbelief and said to myself, "This girl is really crazy."

"He takes me to my doctor's appointments, he does things for me. That little stuff you can do on your own. Plus, while I am over here staying with him, I can save some money."

I said, "You must not be saving too much money if you had to pawn your car."

"He doesn't have that much money because his ex-wife gets all of his money," Lynn said.

"Can't you see that this man can't do anything for you?" I asked her, but she chose to stay stuck in the illusion.

"We are starting a family."

"On what foundation for your building to stand on?"

"I don't want to get married again, I lost my daughter last time in the divorce and I will never get married again," she explained.

"If all you wanted was some kids, you should have got the kids and went on your way. That family or those lives you are trying to build don't have a foundation for a building to stand on. When you have no foundation, anything could come and knock it down," I said.

"He told me he loved me the other day," she said.

I said, "You need to make him prove it because the truth is generally seen and rarely is it heard." Lynn is living a lie or an illusion and people who lack consciousness will even lie to themselves. The truth is, or the reality is, that she has nothing.

It's 9:00 a.m., and my phone rings again.

"Hello?"

"This is Janna, did you watch the news?"

"No!"

"Girrrl, Victoria got burned up in a house fire."

"What! What happened?"

"They said that she fell asleep trying to cook when she came in last night."

Victoria was the type of person to always be in some type of drama. I mean, she was a drama queen. She had been in jail most of her life—she was a booster, a person that steals from the expensive stores and then sells the stolen items. To her this was a way of life, and she thought she was above the law; she had lived this way her entire life. At the end, it all catches up with you.

Tonight I spoke to Steve. He was kind of upset. The house he was trying to get did not come through because when he was younger, he went to prison for selling drugs, and he was unable to get a federal loan because of his criminal background. He said that when the application information came back, all the things he did in his past all came up, like the drug conviction and fighting with the police. All the decisions you make catch up with you at the end, and this is the truth.

We were over at Aunt Valencia's house, and Edward's mother was over there. She was talking about moving out of state. She is emotionally torn because of her son's death. Last night I asked God to give her the strength to pull through. I also asked him to shield my cousins Darren and Troy, to protect them and keep them safe. Darren and Troy have a sister named Lisa. Lisa said, to me let me give you a kiss, cousin; I never got a chance to kiss my brother Edward before he died. Darren, Troy, Lisa and Edward, are all brothers and sisters it's the little things you appreciate after a person is gone. You never know what you have until you lose it. Then you will find that it was everything you were looking for.

I made a phone call to see how Victoria had been doing. Over 80% of her body was burned in the fire—the only thing that didn't get burned in the fire was her feet. She was in the special burn center trying to recover. I remember when she would always bother people, and say bad things to people, or about people. It didn't surprise me that no one had anything good to say about her. Then they found out she got burned. If she pulls through this, maybe she should consider this a wakeup call for her to treat people a little better, and this is true.

Tonight at Lipstix, Child Protection Service called for Goldie. Her son called the police on her—he said that she came in drunk and punched him in the mouth. Rumor around the club is that she always came home drunk and abused her son and that she comes home with many different men. The owner of the club says that it's good that that happened to her, but maybe this will be an eye opener for her to get her life on the right track. Or to maybe try a different type of lifestyle other than that. What's really funny is that when men come into the club, she always says that she is in school. I guess that's to make her look good so she will not feel bad when men ask her how long she's worked there. And when she says 17 years, they will ask if she does anything other than this. They do ask these kinds of questions.

Uncle Charlie is out of jail. He is happy to be home and says he is through drinking, for a little while anyway. He and Liyah are getting along good for now. Today is September 13th, and I have started to get restricted phone calls again. I called my cell phone company to see who keeps playing on my phone, and they said they can't see who is calling me, because when the person who is calling me blocks their number, it's blocked on their network too. The only way to know for sure is to contact the police, but I thought that was a little farfetched. I guess I don't really need the police to tell me who is calling—I have had this phone for seven years, and I have never gotten restricted phone calls so frequently. You know the truth by the way you feel, and the truth doesn't need any proof.

I went to the corner store. I ran into Dana and her husband who saw me pull into the store parking lot and put their van in reverse. She said hi, so I spoke back. I didn't mention anything to her about the letter Maurice had written me where he told me all things she had been saying about me. She asked me for two dollars, and I gave it to her because she must be doing really badly to need two dollars. I asked her where they were going. She said she was going to go to see her daughter in the foster home. I asked her when her daughter was going to be coming back home. Dana said that they gave her six months to get her stuff together. She told me she found a job. It appears to me like they were up to no good. Anyway, I wished her luck with everything. I can see here where she is starting to see the truth or the light that she cannot continue to live her life this way; she should do the right thing just for the sake of her children.

Later that day I ran into her again looking like they were up to the same thing. Then she told me that her 14-year-old son had had a baby while he was in foster care under state custody and that he ran away from the foster home and the state is now looking for him. She told me she was so stressed out and didn't know what to do.

Last night I was on YouTube watching some old cartoons, the coyote and the roadrunner. The coyote was always planning a trap for the roadrunner, and no matter what he planned for the roadrunner, he was always the one to fall into his own trap. It's kind of like my grandfather use to say: when you dig one hole for someone, make sure you dig two, because you don't know who may fall into it first.

Last night Janna called. She said, "Girl, I didn't know that Dana lived in the tower on 24th and B Street. I have a client who lives in the same tower. I was getting off the elevator, and I saw Dana and her husband. Isn't he the reason why she didn't get her kids back?"

My ex-boyfriend Alex is dating some girl. The girl that he is dating called me; I guess she was calling to put me in check about calling her boyfriend. I told her to not call my phone with that crap and left her on the line with the tone. I could not wait until I saw him so I could tell him about himself I Haven't didn't see him for about two months, and when I did, I was with a couple of my girls. I ran into him at the store one day and said, "Damn, dude, why do you have your girlfriend calling my phone?" He was trying to front talking about if it's not about business then don't call. I went off on him and said, "Forget you and your chick. Both of you are throw backs." The truth is that he is mad because I will not sleep with him, and the girl he is dating now is fat and needs to go to the gym. Plus, she needs to clean up her house. After me, he couldn't do any better.

I ran into a guy I had met about seven years ago by the name of Laythen. He is friends with Dana's husband—they grew up together. Laythen went off to college to play football later and then went professional to play in the NFL. Whenever he would come into town, he would always ask my cousin where I was. He had seen pictures of me over at my cousin's house on the wall and would say, "Who is she? Can I meet her?" So they introduced us and that was that. It really amazed me that whenever he would come into town, he would always want to see me. I, on the other hand, was always busy or had to work, so I never got to see him again until one day when Dana called me and told me Laythen wanted to see me. I told her to tell him to come over to Lipstix. When he arrived, I didn't think that he would know who I was because so much time had passed. I saw him come in, so I walked over to him and said hello. He said, "You look different, you look better." I said, "Like wine only gets better with time." So he and I sat down and talked for a while, and we have been hanging out ever since that night. Dana acted like she wanted us to hook up so bad, but later she started trying to ruin me by telling Laythen some stuff about me, things that may or may not have happened in the past. But he couldn't care less. He told her, "Whatever happened then, I didn't know her, so oh well…" She acted mad because he didn't get upset. She later called me to see if I talked to Laythen, and then she tried to tell me things about him. I said to myself, "Why is she telling me this stuff I don't want to know? If he is not being honest with me, it will eventually come out." He thought that I may have done something to her the way she was slandering me which was the same thing Maurice said she was doing to me when he wrote me that letter.

Laythen said that he was looking to make me his wife, and that sounded like music to my ears. It was exactly what I needed.

But you know when you first meet a person, it's always the illusion—the reality may be something totally different. When you get your mind set on what you want, out of nowhere it shows up in your life. Remember, what you think about, you bring about. I guess I am going to see what he is about.

Eight months had passed since I mailed the stuff back to that guy I used to date. What do you know, I opened up my email and saw a message from him with a photo of himself in his boxers and no shirt. He said he was thinking about us. I wrote him back and said that I think about us too. I thought I should be nice and respond as if the little incident never even registered, because naturally people expect for you to respond angrily. When you don't, they will be hesitant to act that way again because they know it requires a response from you, and when you don't give them one, they wonder why you aren't mad. So after that I didn't hear anything else from him. Then a month passed, and I got another email from him with a picture of his nine-year-old daughter on her birthday riding in a limo. I thought to myself, "Why does he keep emailing me? Why doesn't he just go and leave me alone?" To me is seems like he didn't make a conscious decision of what he wanted, and when he realized it, it was too late for him to choose the right to decide. Well… that's just too bad. A lesson learned for him. I guess next time he will know the difference.

My mom called me from down in Arkansas. She asked me if I can come and get her, and said that she needed a break and wanted to come stay with me for a while, so I went to get her. My aunt Valencia and I took the 10 hour drive. When we got there, I went to Denise's house as I hadn't seen her since she came up to visit when we had to attend the funeral. Valencia and I stayed at her house that night. The next day Valencia was disappointed with Denise because Denise had this guy by the name of James that lives with her, and he didn't have a plan or seem to know which direction he was headed. From the looks of it, Denise keeps dealing with losers and expecting different results.

Ring, ring!

"Hello?"

"Hi, this is Laythen."

"Oh! Hi!"

"I have a couple movies that I got, and I was going to stop over so we can watch them." I am on my way back into town; meet me at my house around 10:00 pm. Laythen shows up. He said that on his way over, he stopped by Dana and her husband's house. Her husband just recently got out of jail for domestic violence for supposedly hitting Dana. When he went to jail, she moved out and got her own house, and she destroyed her husband's house. She poured bleach all over the blue carpet, then she turned the air conditioner on. Let me tell you that this is in the winter season. She then turned the water faucet on and left it running for three weeks, the entire time he was in jail. On top of that, she broke the key off into the lock so no one could get into the house.

Today we were all was over to Aunt Valencia's house. I was going over there to see the family. When I walked in, they were talking about Edward, and Edward's mom was saying that her son Darren was telling her that Edward came to him in a dream, and he was crying saying that he did not do anything, this time. Then she said that Darren said Edward came to him one other time and was trying to tell him the name of a person. She then told us about a psychic lady, and when she went to see her, she had a picture of Darren, Troy, and Edward—all three of her sons. She never told the lady anything. All she did was pull the picture out and say, "What can you tell me about these three guys?" The lady touched the picture, and she kind of snatched her hand back fast and pointed at Edward and said, "He is deceased, and he has recently died." This was around the time when he was murdered, and his mom was trying to get answers because the detectives did not have enough information. The psychic also told her that it was someone that he hangs out with and that he was not well liked, they just dealt with him because he would try to buy their friendship, so to speak. She said that they were in a dark colored old, school car and that they had been planning to kill him. It was more than one guy but only one pulled the trigger. She said that there is someone having dreams and to pay attention to the dreams. I can see here were the guy had been thinking of killing Edward, when you think about something long enough, it will soon be a reality. Remember that your thoughts are reality and reality are your thoughts; so does a man think it in his heart, so is he. You know your body doesn't have a mind of its own; it does what your mind tells it to. The things that people hold to in their thoughts are the things that become a reality.

I called Blue today. Blue is another young lady that I know who also works at Lipstix. I had not talked to her in a while, so I called to see what she had been doing. She said she was still working at Lipstix and that business is so-so. Then she told me that Goldie came home one night and caught her boyfriend in the bed with her 16-year-old daughter. Her daughter just recently had an abortion, which makes me wonder whether the baby was her little 16-year-old boyfriend's or her mom's boyfriend's.

"Well, Blue, I'm on my way to work, so I will talk with you later."

"Okay! Bye bye!"

It's Friday, and I think I want to go out and have a drink, so I meet Blue and a couple of other people at this club called Hanks. We were having a good time, then I ran into Maurice's daughter, and she said, "You know, my dad gets out of prison in 60 days. He asked me if I have seen you." I thought to myself, "I hope he don't get out of prison and think that we are going to finish where we left off." I have seen so many people go to prison and get out and be on the same page as they were on when they first left. And if that's what he is on, I don't want any part of that lifestyle. Then Blue started to tell me that when she was at Lipstix, Goldie's boyfriend came in there and hit Goldie in the eye and then he snatched her wig off in front of some customers that she was sitting with. Blue said she was so embarrassed. She was more embarrassed getting her wig snatched off more so than getting hit in her eye.

I stopped at Burger King to get some food and ran into Jo. She said, "Hi! I lost your number. I want to call you and get my hair done." So I give her a card with my shop information on it and told her to call me. Then I asked how her mom was doing. She said, "I don't live with my mom. You know my mom is crazy." Jo is Goldie's 16-year-old daughter. She said she lives with her stepfather. Blue said that the Goldie's boyfriend did not get caught sleeping with the daughter. The daughter's boyfriend had given her some type of venereal disease, and she didn't want her mom to know, so that's why they were looking funny when she had come into the house.

Knock! Knock!

"Who is it?"

"Darren!"

"What's up?"

"I am just stopping by to get my clothes I left over here."

"What you been doing, nothing?"

"I keep having dreams about Edward."

CHAPTER 7: SEED TIME AND HARVEST

We all like reaping good benefits, but we have to be aware of what kind of seeds we are sowing. Weather you believe it or not, we all are sowers, and we carry a hoe everywhere we go. We plant seeds so we reap what we sow, and we plant seeds with what we think. Remember, because you are the one doing the thinking, you are the one who get the reflection. The Bible says in Galatians, 6:7 "be not deceived; God is not mocked, for whatsoever a man soweth that also shall he reap." In Genesis 8:22, it says, "While the earth remains seedtime and harvest, cold and heat, summer and winter, and day and night shall not cease. These are the spiritual laws that are set forth by God; I don't know anyone who lives above this law.

The phone rings, it is 7:00 a.m.

"Hello! Are you awake?"

"Who is this?"

"This is Liyah."

"Hey! What's up?"

"Nothing. You know your Uncle Charlie didn't come home last night."

"What!"

"He has been doing this for quite some time now."

"Really?"

"Yes," she said.

"Well, looks like your relationship has run its course, and it's time to move on. I haven't talked to Uncle Charlie in a long time. I am sorry to hear that. Well… talk to you later.

"Okay, bye!"

I went over to my Aunt Valencia's. Uncle Charlie was over there. I asked him what was wrong with Liyah. He said that she told him that she hated him. She said, "I can't stand you, you ugly mother------." You know the rest. He said that he is tired of her, and it's time to move on, so Uncle Charlie has met someone else. I remember when Uncle Charlie met Liyah when he was married. Uncle Charlie and his wife were on the verge of splitting up when he had started to date Liyah, and she said, "I will take your husband." Well … seed time and harvest, whatever you sow you shall also reap in due season. The same way she got him is the same way she lost him. It started off wrong from the beginning. Another call is coming in on the other line.

"Hello, this is Darryl.

"What's up?"

"You know I got shot?"

"What!?"

"I went by my ex–wife's house to talk to her about some guy she was seeing and the guy used to be a friend of both of ours. When she and I were talking, it kind of led to a slight argument, then my step-son got out of the car and said, 'I told you to stop talking crap to my mother and my sister,' and I turned around and said, 'Dude, it's none of your business.' So I turned back around and continued to talk with my ex–wife. 'Then my step-son said, 'I'm going to tell you one more time to leave my mother and my sister alone.' I repeated that it was none of his business, and just when I turned around he pulled out a gun and shot me in the chest, the arm, and the leg."

I said, "Wow! He really tried to kill you!"

Darryl planted bad seeds, so he just reaping what he sowed. The Bible says in Galatians 6:8, "for he that soweth to his flesh reap corruption; but he that soweth to the spirit reap everlasting life. Let's take a moment and distinguish the two. When you hear the term "flesh," that simply is a way of thinking that opposes what God said, and when you hear the term "spirit," that means a way of thinking that lines up with what God has said, and that you agree with and do what God has said. In John 6:63, it says, "For the flesh profits nothing. But these words that I speak to you are spirit and they are life." In Luke 8:11, it says, "The parable is this, the seed is the word of God." If you have bean seeds and you want to grow beans, what do you need to do with the seed? So is the word of God. So you will never receive any of God promises if you don't plant his word in your heart. Remember, so does a man think it in his heart so is he. The two work together, the heart and the mind. One cannot work without the other.

Here is another letter from Maurice. Let's see what he is talking about. In his letter, he says that he would be in the halfway house in July. A halfway house is a center where you go to get yourself back together before they let you back into society after being incarcerated. Maurice was wondering if he could see me, and if we were still friends. Knowing Maurice, he wants more than just a friendship. Then he started to talk about something in his letter that indicated to me that he is going to get out of prison after spending 15 years of his life there, and do the same thing he did to go to prison in the first place. I don't know if I should respond to his letter because he is one of those type of men who thinks when he gets home, everything is like it was when he left. Years have passed, and one thing I know that is for certain is change. After moving forward, it's hard to look backward.

The phone beeps someone is calling.

"Hello?"

"This is Angel, I was calling to see if I could make a hair appointment."

"Sure! I have an opening at 5:00 p.m."

"What have you been up to?"

"Not much, just working, doing hair, trying to stay busy. What about you?"

"Well… you know they cut my hours down and my pay due to the recession."

"Well, at least you still have a job."

Angel is my ex–boyfriend Alex's sister. I ask, "How is Alex doing? Have you talked to him?" She said that he and his girlfriend had been into an argument, fight, or something to that effect, and the girl will not let him get a breath. She follows him around everywhere he goes, and he is getting tired of it. I find it funny because that's how he used to be with me. Whatever a man sows, also shall he reap in due season.

Another letter from Maurice. He said that he has been locked up for 15 years and doing the time was not easy. He will be going to the halfway house July, that's three months from now. He also said that while he was in prison, he felt a lot of loneliness and despair. Whenever you don't make good decisions, you will make a bad decision, and bad decisions always lead to a lesson of hardship and despair. It's just reaping what you have sowed. I wish I could explain the intricate details on how reaping and sowing works—it's no different from you casting corn seeds in the ground, and after you cast the seeds in the ground, it grows and turns from seed to a stalk of corn. Then you get your harvest, and it's always more than what you put in the ground.

CHAPTER 8: BLURRY VISION

I regain consciousness from blurry vision, and I realize that getting involved with someone who has blurry vision is one if the worst things you can do. If you have no vision, no goal, then you can't go any further than you can see, and it's like you are at a standstill, stuck, not able to go any further because you can't see. When your eyes are open and your reality is still blurry, then you need some help. In Proverbs 29:18, it says, "Where there is no vision people perish."

Ring!

"Hello?"

I just got a phone call and the person on the other end told me that one of my uncles just died. I could not believe it. Well... I guess I have to attend another funeral. At the funeral, I just looked at my uncle, and he looked like a clay like figure, which brought to mind Genesis 2:7. "And the Lord God formed man of dust of the ground, and breathed into his nostrils the breath of life; and man became a living soul." Without God's breath of life in man, he is nothing but dirt. In Ecclesiastes 12:7, it says, then shall the dust return to the earth as it was; and the spirit shall return unto God who gave it." I don't understand how you can have blurry vision when the truth is generally seen and rarely is it heard.

Lynn called me to give me her condolences about my uncle. She started to say she was ready to move out of the house with her boyfriend. She is coming to the realization that her building is not going to hold up because she doesn't have a solid foundation for it to stand on, and her vision is coming clear. I stopped by Lipstix to see Goldie. I was going to invite her to my going away party, but they said she no longer worked there. I ran into this girl named Bird who is a member of the church we all attend, and she said that Goldie has been at church. She stopped the drugs and drinking, and she really looked great. Her vision is starting to be clear.

Well... Uncle Charlie is back in jail due to another domestic dispute for fighting with Liyah. This time I don't think he will be getting out of jail anytime soon. While he was in jail, she sold everything in the house, took the kids, and moved to Denver. When he does get out of jail, he will not have a home to go to, and he and Liyah have been fighting and arguing for about six years. I get so tired of hearing about that mess. Whenever he calls me to try and talk about it, I cut him off and tell him I don't want to hear that. He is just like that dog sitting on that nail, and he keeps moaning. He has been dealing with that drama for six years or more, and at the end, he didn't gain anything. The Bible says in John 6:63, "For the flesh profits nothing: the words I speak unto you, are spirit, and they are life."

Maurice called. He has got out of prison and is in the halfway house. Just when he was getting out, I was packed up and ready to leave and move back to Memphis, so I went to see him and took him to a couple of his appointments. He thought that we were going to sleep together. I just don't feel the same way. Plus, he has been locked up for 15 years, and there is no telling what he has been doing in there. To be honest, I was extremely happy to be leaving when he was getting out. He was going to invite himself into my life no matter what I said. Then he start talking about how he was going to transfer his parole to Arkansas or Memphis, and when he said that, I instantly felt bad for thinking that I don't want to be bothered with that, so I just told him and he stopped calling. I guess his vision is clear, and he finally saw that I am not interested in being with him. Right before I was getting ready to leave, Laythen stopped by. He was really annoying that day, and I said something to him and he went off on me. So I told him to have a nice evening and never called him again. I knew then that he was bitter with women because when he was playing football. He had a wife and when she found out he was not going to play football the next season, she left him. He kidnapped her at gun point and ended up going to prison for eight years. My vision is clear: if I would have dealt with him, I would have been miserable.

Denise just called me and gave me some horrible news. Liyah has been going hard. Uncle Charlie is in jail, and she is one of those women who can't make it on her own, so now she is on drugs, and she had some junkies around the little kids and the kids got raped.

Well… I have moved now. I am in Memphis, Tennessee. Now I can breathe again, a brand new start is what I needed. Dear readers, guess what? You know the guy I was dating, the one who lived in another state? He got a message from me that I left with his sister. I told her to tell him to stop calling my phone. I know that it's him, and I have moved out of state. Besides, I am getting married in March. Do you know that he popped up on me saying how sorry he was and how much he misses me and how he wants to try it again. I explained to him that I don't want to be his girlfriend. And if he wanted girlfriends, he can do that. I, on the other hand, don't want to be bothered with that because there is nothing to be gained in that. All he does is waste time, and at the end, he gained nothing. John 6:63 says, "For the flesh profits nothing." I guess after us being apart for two years, he realized what he had after I was gone.

My phone is ringing off the hook. Everybody I know from the Omaha a city where I use to live is calling me telling me that the owner of Hanks has died. I was devastated because Hanks was one of those places you would go to see everybody when you come to town to visit. His woman he had been with for 19 years never married him, so when he died, she had no say over anything. She gained nothing. I hope this gives her a clear vision. Had she followed the instruction manual, she would have gained something, but all she did was waste time and at the end she had nothing.

CHAPTER 9: SPIRITUAL DEATH

To be carnal-minded is death, but to be spiritual-minded is peace. Uncle Charlie and Aunt Valencia came to town to visit. They wanted to come see how everything was going since I had moved. When they were here, Denise and James got into an argument about some toilet paper and dish washing liquid. Denise said she was tired of not having anything with James. She said James doesn't like to provide for his family, and he treats everyone nice but Denise. She has to argue with him about little things like toilet paper and dish soap even though he lived there too, and he eats out of the same dishes. So she told him to get out of her house. I don't like to get into anyone's business but it doesn't seem that James has a relationship with God, and that says enough by itself. When Denise gets up on Sunday to go to church, he never goes with her. He doesn't plan on doing anything right. A man without God is spiritually dead anyway. In II Corinthians 6:14, it says, "Be ye not unequally yoked with unbelievers; for what fellowship has rightness with unrighteousness? And what has light with darkness?

Uncle Charlie said that Liyah was in jail for child abuse. When she went back to Denver, she started abusing the kids. She has a history of child abuse on her record; I don't know how her situation may turn out. Now Uncle Charlie has to get an attorney to try and get custody of his kids.

"Hey! Aunt Valencia, how are you? Did you have a safe trip?"

"Yes, I did! Have you talked to Dana?"

"I saw her about a week ago, she had bought a cute little car, if her husband don't tear it up for her. You know, I heard she works at the truck stop."

"Well, that's good she found something to do."

"No! I mean working at the truck stop."

"Are you serious?"

"Yep! That's what hear. I hope she is not doing that. It's dangerous. She can't possibly be in her right mind."

"Is she still on drugs?"

"I think she may be."

Well…that is terrible. In Romans 8:5, it says, "Those that are after the flesh do mind the things of the flesh, those who are after the spirit mind the things of the spirit." Remember how to distinguish the two, flesh and spirit. In John 6:63, it tells us that "for the flesh profits nothing: And people wonder why they aren't any further than they are in life, and they say where all my years went? They spent so much time walking in the flesh, that when they realized it, life was almost over and at the end they never gain anything.

Ring, ring!

"Hello? Who is this?"

"This is Angel."

"Hey! What's up girl?"

"Nothing much. Just wanted to know how your Thanksgiving was."

"It was great. I was with my family this year, and it was wonderful to be at my mom's on the holiday. How was yours?"

"Well… I cooked a little. I didn't go over to anybody's house this year; I stayed home and did my own thing."

"Hello?"

"Hey! This is Darren, how are you?"

"I am okay. How is Troy?"

"Troy went to jail for drinking and driving under suspension. This is his sixth offense, so he might be going to prison. I hate to say it, but it might be a good place for him because it will keep him out of trouble and from getting drunk every day. How is it in Memphis?"

"I love it. It's a change of scenery for a while. Plus, I am home with my mom, sisters, and brother."

"You know, I have been thinking about leaving here myself. I miss you now that you are gone. I would always have somewhere to go when you were here, but now I just don't do much of anything."

"Well, you can always come and visit."

Janna is calling. Beep!

"What's up, girl?"

"Nothing. How is everything going?"

"Everything is going is great! How about you?"

"I need a vacation."

"Well, you can always come to visit me when you get ready."

"Oh, you know Maurice went back to jail for violating his curfew in the halfway house."

"Didn't I tell you when he was writing me those letters, when he was getting ready to get released, in his letters he had said something that indicated that he was going to get out and do the same thing."

"Yep! You sure did."

I knew he was on some B.S. He is still the same, still dead in his spirit. If you do not follow the instructions that God has left us, then you will remain dead in your spirit. In James 1:22, it says, "But be doers of the word and not hears only, deceiving yourself. For if anyone is a hearer of the word and not a doer he is like a man who looks at his natural face in a mirror, for he looks at himself and go away and at once forgets what manner of man he was." After taking a glance at the mirror, and you get to take a look at yourself, if you don't make any changes, then you will continue to get the same results. He is clearly deceiving himself.

I just woke up this morning getting ready to go to the beauty shop, and I took a glance at my cell phone and saw that I missed a phone call at 2:30 a.m. I also noticed that was an area code from where the guy I used to date has called. I thought to myself, because it was a Friday night, he probably was drunk and started feeling some type of a way. Then he called back at 7:30 a.m.

"Hello?"

He said, "I have been calling you all night, I need you to come to Illinois and come and get me. I am in trouble. I need to come live with you for a minute. I will tell you the rest in person."

I said, "Okay. I will leave on Sunday morning at 8:00 a.m."

On Sunday, I left to go get him and arrived in Illinois at 5:00 p.m. We turned right around and left, getting back to my place at 2:00 a.m. I continue to go on with my everyday life, and he was at my place for two weeks. Then one Friday night at about 8:00 p.m., we were getting ready to step out for a while and have a drink and discuss a few things, so I took a shower. He had just taken his shower, and while I was getting dressed, the doorbell rang. I said, "Who is it?"

"The police!"

I responded, "The police?"

I opened the door and the officer said, "Ma'am,, do you know this man?" He showed me a picture, and while I was looking at the picture of the guy I used to date, I also noticed my house was surrounded with FBI agents.

He said, "You are in no trouble, but the guy you are with has a federal warrant." They arrested him and took him to jail. Life is funny. I remember when I wanted to live with him and do something a little different, he stopped answering the phone, and now he has to call me. The same people you meet on your way up, you meet on your way down. So trying to be his friend, I put money in his account, and unblocked my phone so he could call and get a message through. My sister thinks I shouldn't do anything for him. She said, "The way he did you, I would not speak to him again." In Romans 12:20, it says, "If your enemy is hungry, feed him; if he thirst, give him a drink for in doing so thou shalt heap coals of fire on his head. Be not overcome of evil but overcome evil with good." He is probably sitting in jail wishing he would have made a conscious decision of what he wanted, because he didn't, and a choice was made for him. Now he is realizing what he wanted was to live, but now it is too late. In Proverbs 14:12, it says, "There is a way that which seem right unto a man, but the end thereof are the ways of death even in laughter the heart is sorrowful; and at the end of that mirth is heaviness.

I guess the turtle always catches up with the rabbit eventually.

CHAPTER 10: GUARD YOUR HEART

In Proverbs 4:20, it says, "My son attend to my words; incline thine ear unto my saying let them not depart from your eyes; keep them in the midst of thine heart for they are life for those that find them and health to all their flesh. Keep thy heart with all diligence; for out of it are the issues of life." The mind and the heart work together; one cannot work without the other.

Ring, ring!

"Hello?"

"You have a collect call from Briggs at the Grady County Federal Detention Center. To accept this call, dial one now."

"Hey, Briggs! How are you? Sorry about your situation."

"I need for you to look in that bag that I left at your apartment and get this book out of it and send it to my sister so she can give it to my attorney. I just want to say thank you and that I appreciate everything you have done for me."

The operator said, "You have one minute remaining."

"Well, Briggs, the phone is going to hang up, call me later."

"Okay, bye."

I went through the bag, and guess what I found in it?

Ring, ring! Another call is coming in.

"Hello?"

"Hey, this is Bella. I am going to leave Atlanta on Friday."

"Okay! I will see you when you get here."

Bella is my cousin who lives in Atlanta, and she is coming to Memphis to meet me so we can go to my nephew's graduation. In the meantime, I went through the bag and I found 10 ounces of marijuana and some discharge papers from the hospital. The girl that Briggs was dating was over three months pregnant, but never told me anything about it. At this point, I was very angry with him for not telling me he had drugs in my house and a baby on the way. On top of that, I was trying to look out and be a friend to him. What if the United States Marshalls would have searched my house? I said to myself, "After all this time, you come around still on the same bull." I couldn't wait until he calls back.

Bella is here in town, and we are getting ready to go back to Omaha a city I use to live. When I got into town, my friend Steve had reserved me a hotel at the casino. He said, "I know you are going to be kicking it with your family, so when you get tired of them, you can go get away."

"Thanks, Steve, that's really thoughtful of you" I told him.

It had been 10 months since I moved, and after going back, I was glad I did. It was really nice to see a lot of people I knew. I was at the gas station and ran into Maurice.

"What's up, Maurice? How have you been?"

"I have been good, how about you?"

"I am doing great!"

"How are you liking Memphis?"

I replied, "I am loving it. Hey, I am on my way to my Aunt Valencia's house. You should stop by there a little later. She lives off of 36th Street. You should see a silver Lexus with Tennessee plates on the car."

"Okay, I will. Talk with you later."

When I get to Valencia's, Dana was over there. She was living in an upstairs bedroom. It was good to see her, but she had made no progress. In fact, I felt sorry for her decision she has made.

Knock, knock. Someone is at the door, and it's Maurice. He stopped by my aunt's house to see me. Remember, Maurice is the one who had been in prison for 15 years, and he had not changed one bit. He and I ran to get something to eat. On the way, he said, "I have to make another stop if you don't mind." I replied, "I am riding with you." He stopped at some house. A guy came out, got in the car, and gave Maurice some money in exchange for drugs. After the guy got out of the car, I asked Maurice, "Didn't you just get out of prison for that same stuff?" He never said anything; he just looked kind of dumbfounded in the face. When I got back to Valencia's, we hung around having some wine, laughing, and enjoying the family.

I got a phone call from Briggs' friend Tops. I didn't answer because Briggs only wanted to bug me because now he is in jail and he needs a friend, but when I was trying to be his friend, he sold me out. And for some reason, when it comes to me, his intentions are never good. He has no life, and dead people with no life crave it, so they look for someone full of life to kill their spirit too. Besides, I was on vacation and did not want to die from someone else's misery. I only had one more day to hang out before I had to get back to Memphis, so I was planning to use that day to try and see all of my old buddies.

Well, it is Monday morning, and it is time to gas up the car and hit the highway. I have a ten-hour drive back to Memphis. Finally, Bella and I made it back—what a long drive. It's time to get some sleep and get ready to go to the beauty shop so I can tend to my clients. It's 8:00 p.m. and my phone is ringing. It's Tops calling again, and at this point. I am very irritated.

"Hello!"

"Where are Briggs' clothes, computer, and all the things he left at your house?"

I politely hung up my phone and blocked his number. I didn't want to hear about anything concerning Briggs. In John 14:27, it says, "Peace I leave with you, my peace I give unto you; not as the world giveth, give I unto you let not your heart be troubled neither let it be afraid." So I have a choice, because it clearly says "let not your heart be troubled," and that word troubled means characterized by unrest or disorder, distress, affliction, danger or troubled areas. So remember to guard your heart because the issues of life flow from it. Briggs is in jail, on his way to prison, and he cannot wear the clothes nor can he use a computer. He is just looking for someone to drag down.

CHAPTER 11: THE ADVERSARY

The Bible says that the devil, Satan, is your adversary and that makes him the enemy of our soul. It is written that he looks to devour your soul, which is your mind area. Remember, so does a man think it in his heart so is he. In 1 Peter 5:8, it says, "Be sober, be vigilant; because your adversary the devil, as roaring lion, walks about, seeking whom he may devour; That word vigilant means careful, observant, or attentive in your thinking because the devil will try to devour us by coming in a disguise to deceive us—he would use any method. How can we see through these disguises? By judging the tree by its fruit—a good tree brings forth good things, and a bad or evil tree bring forth bad things. The fruit just means the things that are going on in their lives, so when the devil shows up, he comes through people, and it depends on what spirit they have inside of them. Some people have a perception of the devil as a monster with horns and a pitchfork, but that is so far from the truth. The devil appears through the people we encounter on daily basis. Everything is not as it seems or appears to be, so you have to look closely to see the things that are not seen. It's up to us to know the difference.

I just arrived at the beauty shop, and there's a letter from Briggs waiting for me. In his letter he was saying that the feds would be coming to my job and that they know I sold some weed. He tried to do anything he could do to pull me down, so I never responded to the letter. I figure the best way to handle this situation is whatever you do, do not respond. People like Briggs cannot drag you down in the long run. And when you don't respond, it lets you know what a person's true intentions are.

The phone is ringing. I have a phone call from my cousin Dana. She called to tell me that her brother was shot six times at a nightclub. This guy by the name of Jughead that used to hang out with Dana's brother was killed execution style. This girl by the name of Marie is Jughead's sister who came into the nightclub and saw Dana's brother in there. She called her other brother by the name of Eric to let him know that Dana's brother was inside the nightclub and said it was their time to get him back for killing

Jughead. So the people came in shooting, thinking Dana's brother had something to with Jughead getting killed. They were looking to get revenge. Surprisingly, Dana's brother survived the six gun shots. And hopefully he will make a change for the better. As for Eric, he was killed in the midst of trying to get revenge for his brother, and now Marie now has two dead brothers. When you dig one hole, make sure you dig two.

Ring!

"Hello?"

"Hey, Steve, how are you?"

"I am doing well. Happy New Year."

"Happy New Year to you too! What's been going on with you?"

"Well, I just want to say thank you for being such a good friend. I was just sitting here thinking to myself that everything you told me a long time ago I wish I would have listen to you then. Now I am just starting to figure it out. I have to admit I was so foolish, I didn't recognize a blessing when it was looking me in the face. I am also glad you begged me to stop hanging with Jughead. You heard about what happened to him, didn't you?"

"Yeah, I heard, and it is terrible."

"I was thinking that could have been me running with that click when that happened. You know, I have become the deacon of the church I've been attending."

"That's great, Steve. I am so proud of you."

"I just wish I would have listened to you a long time ago."

"Well, it's not how you start the game; it's how you finish it. You first have to realize you're losing in order to win. It's sad when you're losing and don't realize it. At least I can say you realized you were losing so you can start to win. I am getting ready for bed. I have to go to the salon tomorrow and tend to my clients, so call me later."

"Okay! Goodnight."

I get to the salon the next day and take a lunch break about 5:00 p.m. My receptionist said, "Some guy called for you. I told him you were on lunch. He asked if you were working today, and I said you were here until 8:00 p.m. He asked if you had an email address or a phone number where he could get a hold of you, but I told him that I could not give out that kind of information." I told my receptionist to push *69 to get the phone number to see where the call was coming from, and what do you know? Mr. Briggs had someone call for him from jail. I just don't want to be bothered with his lies, games, or any of his drama anyway, so I never called the number back. Maybe he will get the picture.

Ring!

"Hello?"

"Who is calling?"

"This is Ashley."

"Hi, how have you been?"

"I have been okay."

"I haven't talked to you in a month of Sundays. Are you still in love with Dupree?"

"Yes! You know he moved in."

"What! That's why I haven't heard from you. You didn't quit until you got him in the house with you. How is that going?"

"Well, it was going good at first, but then I ran into some financial difficulties and he had to pay for everything. He has this wishy-washy attitude. You never really know a person until you get in the house with them, and even then, you can be with a person for years and never really know them. Eventually their true colors will come out, then you will say to yourself, 'I didn't sign up for this,' and often more than not, by the time you realize it, it's too late. You have given up too much; it's like sleeping with the enemy, the devil. So when are you coming to visit?"

"I am supposed to visit sometime in February, around the 13th. I need a vacation. I am going to book a flight this time because I don't want to take a 10-hour drive by myself. I need a break from the salon as well, so mark your calendar for the 13th through the 19th. I will see you when I get there, and I will talk with you later."

The 13th arrived, and it was time to go. I arrived into town and slept over at my Aunt Valencia's a couple of nights before I checked into my hotel. This way I could hang out with friends and family before I got some me time. I called Steve to let him know that I was at my Aunt Valencia's house and to tell him to come over. He said, "I will call you when I get myself together." "Okay! Talk with you later," I responded.

I stopped by Blue's house to see what was going on with her. We laughed and reminisced and drank a glass of Barefoot Moscato.

"It's getting late, blue. I think I better take off. What are you going to do for the rest of the evening?"

"I have to go to work."

"Where do you work now?"

She says, "I still work at the club."

"Are you still dancing?"

"Yes, I am."

"Okay, Blue, I will see you later."

Ring, ring!

"Hello? Who is this?"

"This is Liyah"

"Hey girl! How have you been? I haven't talked to you in a long time. How is Denver? What are you doing now?"

"I have not been doing so good, I am in the rehab center trying to pick up the pieces of my life; I don't know where to begin. I just sit here and look at myself and I realize how I have ruined my children's lives. The kids are in state custody. You remember my oldest son, the gay one, Ray?"

"Yes, I remember him."

"Well, he has AIDS."

"That is horrible."

"So I am in here to trying to get them back."

"Liyah, I am so sorry about your situation."

"Have you talked to your Uncle Charlie?"

"As a matter of fact I have. I talked to him right before I left town. You know he lives in Memphis now with his girlfriend."

CHAPTER 12: FROM THE INVISIBLE TO THE VISIBLE

When something is invisible, it is withdrawn from our sight or hidden. In Luke 8:17, it says, "For nothing is secret, that shall not be made manifest neither anything hid, that shall not be known and come aboard." Let's look at the word manifest. It means "clearly revealed to the mind or the senses."

Ring!

"Hello? Hey Steve! How are you?"

"I am doing great!"

"Well, that's good. What's up?"

"The other day I stopped by A.D.'s house and saw Marie over there, and I have to be honest with you, she looked horrible. She has lost all kinds of weight. She has dark circles around her eyes looking like a raccoon. I asked her what was wrong, and she said that she was in the Ale Gent Health Center in the mental institution for trying to commit suicide. Her entire family has turned on her. They said that she called Eric down to the nightclub and got him killed, plus she has to go to court to testify about the shooting in the nightclub. When she was at work, Lamont came up to her job and called her a snitch, embarrassing her in front of her co-workers, and telling her that if she goes to court, they are going to kill her. I felt so sorry for her situation. I told her to come pray with me, I gave her the number to the church, and said she is welcome to come." Do you think she will show up Steve, I replied? I don't know, she is welcome to come is she wants to. Steve replied. Well Steve I have to go, I will chat with you later.

My mom has passed away. She was very sick and had been on dialysis for the last 17 years. She said before she left that this old place was not her home anyway. She also said that she was tired and ready to go home and that she had a right to go home. She told me she loved me and that she was ready to go, so she left. She stepped outside her body and because she was no longer in it, the body just collapsed. Before that all happened, she had flat-lined a few times. I think she got a glimpse of heaven and didn't want come back to this place. In II Corinthians 4:18, it says, "While we look not at the things which are seen, but at the things which are not seen for the things which are seen are temporal; but the things which are not seen are eternal." To me this indicates that there is an unseen realm, and we can't comprehend because we are in a physical form. But when you leave the physical form, you will then be in a spiritual form and can comprehend spiritual matter.

The phone is ringing.

"Hello? Hey Steve."

"I was just calling back to check on you to see how you are holding up."

"Well, Steve, I'm doing okay for the most part, just trying to deal with the harsh reality. She is gone now to a better place. It's all over now, and it seems like I couldn't get any rest until it was all over. My birthday is like a week away, and after all this, I don't really feel much like celebrating."

"Lisa just called and told me that she went out to a cocktail lounge to meet and hang out with a couple of friends, and while she was out, she ran into Marie. She was talking about that shooting that took place at the nightclub where her brother got gunned down, and how she was going to kill Dana's brother when he gets out of jail. Lisa asked her how she knows if he murdered her brother. She replied, 'My brother said if anything happens to me, Coupe did it to me. I owe him my life.' Lisa thought to herself, if he thought he owed Coupe his life, then why is Marie worried about it? I almost told her, 'Well, aren't you the one who told him to come down to the nightclub in the first place? But I just held my tongue. I didn't want to make matters worse, so I didn't say anything.'"

My phone is ringing. I just spoke with Maurice and ask him if he had heard from Dana.

He said, "Dana is living in the Francis House."

"What!"

"The Francis House. The Francis House is a shelter you can go to when you have no place to go."

"What is going on with her?"

"I don't know. Those two cannot seem to get things together."

"When are you coming to visit again?"

"I don't know, maybe when the weather gets better. I don't want to come visit in the snow. Well, Maurice, I have to go. Chat with you later."

The next morning I took a glance at my phone. I had a text message from out of state and I was surprised that it was Dana. I don't know if Maurice called her or what, but ironically, she texted me and said, "Good morning, I love you." I was so shocked because I hadn't heard from her since August. We had a good text exchange, and I didn't mention her situation about living in the Francis House. I was happy to hear from her. I gave her words of encouragement to try and lift her up a little bit. I told her that sometimes you need to leave people behind because they will drag you down, especially if they don't want anything. They will keep you from getting it, and by the time you realize it or their intentions, it's too late. You have to know the different when dealing with people; it's not the people, but the spirit that lives inside them that you battle against. In Ephesians 6:12, it says, "For we wrestle not against flesh and blood, but against principalities, against powers, against the rulers of darkness of this world, against wickedness in high places." You need to get your spirit strong again. You have to keep your spirit fed with the word of God, because the word is spirit. Just like your physical body needs food, your spirit does too. When you don't feed your spirit and it is life, it dies just like if you didn't feed your physical body—it would die too. All we are is a spirit that possesses a soul that lives in a physical body. Our spirit is what keeps us alive.

After sharing this message with my Dana she said, "Thank you, because I needed to hear those words of encouragement."

"You are welcome. Stay in touch. I love you. Text me later."

Its 1:00 a.m. on Saturday night, and my phone is going crazy with texts. I look at the message, it's from my sister Denise. It says, "Pick up, it's important." So I call her back. She says, "Come over quick, James is trying to fight me." I hung up after saying I'd be there in a minute. I arrive shortly at my sister's house, she and James have gotten into some sort of disagreement about something stupid, both of them where drunk and had been up all night with a house full of people. The police had arrived they were getting ready to take both of them to jail, for disorderly conduct. Lucky no one went to jail that night. I returned home to get ready to leave town for the family reunion.

It's the Fourth of July, and I'm on my way to St. Louis to a family reunion. I'm so excited because I am going to meet my

Aunt Valencia there. She is going to ride back to the Omaha with me after the reunion is over, and I am going to stay at her house for a while before I make my way back to Memphis. This will also give me a chance to see some of my old buddies. I called Steve when I got into town. He was so excited to see me, and I was happy he was doing really well for himself. I hung with Lynn, my childhood friend, the entire time I was there. She had bought herself a new Hummer truck. It was really nice and stylish. She still is a little off the wall in her thinking.

My cell phone is ringing,

"Hey, this is Ashley. Did you make it into town yet?"

"Yes! As a matter of fact, I did. So what's up?"

"Nothing much. I just spoke to Alex he wants to see you."

"Okay, well, give him my number and have him give me a call."

"Okay, talk to you later."

I went over to Dana's house. She looked not too good. She was on her way to court for some robbery she was involved with. This girl just loves drama or something because she is always in some type of conflict. She will never get her children back unless they decide to deal with her on their own. Besides, they are practically all grown up now. While I was over there, Maurice showed up.

"Hey! When did you get into town?"

I replied, "Yesterday."

"You look like you've been taking care of yourself."

I smiled and said, "Did you expect anything else?"

I have to be honest. This is one man that will not leave the street life alone. If he gets in trouble again, he probably will never get out of prison.

He said, "You can come over to my house and stay if you like."

"Oh! That's so nice of you, but no thanks." I thought to myself, "What if I go over there and someone kicks the door in? You know, people who live like this will get you killed."

"Well, it was nice seeing you all, but I have to go now because I have so many people I need to see and not a lot of time to do it."

"Oh! By the way, has anyone heard from coupe?"

Maurice replied, "Yes, he is getting ready to get out of prison. I saw Marie. She was talking trash saying, 'I'm going to kill coupe, he killed both my brothers.'"

I head over to Blue's house to see what she has been up to. She said that she was not dancing anymore. Some girls at the club tried to set her up with some prostitution sting or something like that. She was in the VIP room giving a lap dance to some guy who happened to be an undercover police. She said he pulled out his private part and she didn't report it, so she got hit with a ticket. I told her that it was for her own good because she probably would still be working in there if that didn't happen.

I got a call from Alex. He was very happy to see me; I haven't seen him in about five years. I hung out with him and had a couple of cocktails, laughed and talked about old times. We went over to my Aunt Valencia's house to continue hanging out for the rest of the evening. Then he started talking about getting back together, and the thought of that instantly made me feel terrible. It was great to see him, but I don't think I could go there again.

My vacation was about over, and I had to get back home to get ready for work. When I got to work, one of the girls I work with said, "Hey, when you were on vacation, an older black guy came here looking for you." I asked her if he wanted a haircut or something, but she didn't think so. I thought it was kind of weird, so I looked at her puzzled trying to figure out who that could have been. She said, "I told him you were on vacation."

About a week after I had been back to work, the guy showed up again.

He walked up to me and said, "Hi."

I said, "Hello. Can I help you?" while I was looking at him, trying to see where I knew him from.

He said, "You and I share a mutual friend."

I said, "Who? What friend?"

He said, "Briggs." I was flabbergasted, speechless. I was shocked. He said, "He told me to tell you that he is home, and he wants you to call him." Then he asked me for my number.

I said, "I will take his number and call him." But I never did call him. I didn't think I really had very much to say to him. Besides, he tried to destroy me.

Ring, ring.

"Hello? Who is this?"

"This is Lisa."

"Oh! Hi, Lisa, how are you?"

"I'm doing quite well. I was just calling to say hello because I haven't talk to you in a while."

"It's really nice to hear from you,"

"You too. My brother Troy is on his way out of prison. He is out now looking for a job. He's on some kind of work release program where they let him out to go to work only, then he has to return back to the halfway house."

"That should be good for him, that way he can see where he will end up next time he decides to make a stupid decision. Plus, he will get a chance to stand on his own to see how it is to be a man. Well, got to go, a call is coming in."

"Hey!" This was my sister Denise.

"I thought you were going to stop by the house."

"I'm on the way."

I arrived over at my sister's, and we got to talking. I glanced at the table and saw a letter from coupe with some photos in it. What was he talking about? He was saying he was thinking of coming this way when he got out. I said to myself, "Not if he is going to live like he has been living." He lives the fast, dangerous life, and if you deal with his kind, you can get yourself in a lot of mess. The holiday is here, and I have family coming here from out of town. I'm so excited! I get to see Dana, Valencia, Uncle Charlie, and a bunch of my other family.

CHAPTER 13: HOW DO I WIN THE FIGHT AGAINST THE ENEMY?

In Ephesians 6:12, it says, "For we wrestle not against flesh and blood, but against principalities, against powers, against the rulers of the darkness of this world, against spiritual wickedness in high places. . ." The family has finally made it into town, and we are getting ready to barbeque, pop fireworks, and enjoy the holiday. Dana got here too, and she is so excited! She has an ex-boyfriend she has not seen in about 10 or 15 years. She hangs out with him and was talking about getting back together, moving, and starting her life over. The whole time she was here she was saying how happy and at peace she was. And that she really didn't want to ride back with Valencia. She said, "I'm done with drugs, I just need a fresh start. Seriously, I am thinking about not going back." So Dana and Denise went to the hotel where they shared a room with double beds. The next morning I spoke with Denise, and I told her to take my spare key and open my door for Valencia. She left some things at my house, and she needed to get them. I was headed to work. Denise said shortly after I spoke with her, she left the hotel to go and let Valencia in the house. She said she told Dana to be ready when she got back because, at that point, it would be time to check out. When she arrived back to the hotel to pick up Dana, she saw Dana's ex-boyfriend from years ago is standing outside crying. At first she thought he was upset because she had changed her mind about getting back together and moving back to be with him, but when she pulled up, he said that she would not wake up, and he thought something was wrong. When she went into the hotel room, she found Dana was dead. They think she may have died as soon as she lay down because rigor mortis had started to set in. The coroner and police arrived, and there were no visible signs of the cause of death, so they had to perform an autopsy and toxicology analysis. In the meantime, everyone was in a state of shock. In such disbelief. Dana's ex-husband paid to have her body shipped back, so we had to drive to attend the funeral. The funeral was a lot of chaos. I had never gone to a funeral where there was so much chaos.

About a week after the funeral, I got a phone call saying that they had seen Dana's son on the news for first degree murder. I don't think he was handling the death of his mother very well. The news said that he tried to rob someone for some money. The man was known around for dealing some type of drugs, and I guess he thought the man had a substantial amount of cash, at least that's what the word was on the streets. So now he was in jail waiting to go to trial.

Ring, ring! The phone is ringing. It's my cousin Lisa.

"Hey, girl, what's up?"

"Nothing much, girl. Guess who just sent me a friend request on Facebook?"

"Who?"

"Briggs, girl."

"Shut up! I don't know how he managed to find you."

"Well, you and I have the same last name. He must have been looking for you, and you don't have Facebook, but he remembered me. He asked me if I was your cousin, and then he said, 'You are that crazy country one.'"

"Wow!" My mouth just hung open. "Wonder what he wants, I haven't heard from him in a long time."

"Well, he just asked how you were doing. I told him you just bought a house and you are about to get married."

My phone is ringing. It's an out of town number, I wonder who this could be.

"Hello?"

"Hey, girl."

"Who is this?"

"This is Monique." Monique is Dana's younger sister. "I was just calling to tell you the toxicology report came back about Dana, and it said that she died because she suffered a seizure in her sleep. There were no drugs in her system."

I guess she was really telling the truth about wanting to move and start over. She had also mentioned how she was through with the drugs. I guess sometimes it is a little too late. I started to wonder whether it was so many years of drugs that caused her to have a seizure, or if it could be a past injury. I remember when

Dana and I were in high school, she started dating this man name Braxton. Everybody told her that he was crazy and he beat women, but Dana wanted to date him anyway. She end up getting pregnant by Braxton, and the son they had together is the son that is in jail for murder. During her pregnancy, he beat her with a nine millimeter handgun. Blood was pouring out of her head like a water faucet. He almost killed her then, but by the grace of God, he didn't. I think that could have caused a brain injury. Braxton went to prison for beating her with the gun. I'm not sure how much prison time he got, but I know it was for a long time.

CHAPTER 14 THE STORM:

A storm is a disturbance of the atmosphere, a sudden occurrence of something in large amounts. It seems to me that we all have some type of storm we have to deal with. Some storms are more visible and people can see what you're going through, and other times there are the silent storms where it seems like no one but you knows it.

Ring!

The phone is ringing. It's my Aunt Valencia, and she just told me that Dana's son is facing a life sentence. Wow, his mother is dead, and now it looks like he is heading to prison for the rest of his life. I can see here where he didn't make a good decision, and his decision changed his destination.

Uncle Charlie had a massive heart attack. He is now on life support; according to the doctors, they have never seen anyone survive this kind of heart attack. Uncle Charlie had high cholesterol, and he was not taking his medicine like he was supposed to. He was in denial that he had this illness, so he decided not to take it and he died.

I didn't attend Uncle Charlie's funeral. I was so tired of going to funerals. They seem to be too frequent. I once heard some say that death comes in threes; I think that may have some truth to it. It appears that family was dying one after another; so instead, I planned a trip to go and visit. I didn't want to go under the circumstances of a funeral—I can't deal with that image staying in my head. That bothers me, so I stayed home.

I did, however, go visit, and it was a fun visit. I wanted to see people I didn't see the last time I came in town. I ran into Goldie, and she looked fantastic. Goldie said I am still attending the church we used to attend together when I lived there. She continued to go after I moved away. She also stopped drinking, has a regular job, and she married the deacon at the church. I told her that I couldn't be more proud and happy for her. Goldie and I hung out for a while and went out to eat—we really had a wonderful time.

The phone is ringing.

"Hello?"

"Hey! This is Steve. I hear you're in town. I am going to stop by and see you."

"Okay! Stop over to Valencia's house," I replied. I always stayed at my Aunt Valencia's house—she was one of my favorite aunts, plus she is so down to earth and super funny. She has a sense of humor out of this world.

Steve arrives. "Hey! It's so good to see you," Steve said.

"It's good to see you too, Steve," I replied back.

"Hey, let's go check out my new house," Steve said.

"I would love to," I replied. I was really impressed with his home. It was so nice and big. "How much did you spend to get this?"

Steve replied, "Around $125,000."

"This is a very nice home, Steve," I replied. "I remember you were trying to purchase a home a couple of years ago, and it was very hard for you with the felonies and different things going on. After coming out of the storm, you have your answer that all things work out in time and in season. You have to endure the storm first, so when it finally happens, you will very much appreciate it. Remember the old saying "no pain no gain."

Steve replied, "I have to be honest with you. I wish I would have listened to you a long time ago. When I was running the streets, I thought I was gaining something. I had a pocket full of drug money and all the women I could imagine, but when it was all over, I had nothing. I went to prison for a long time, all the women were gone, and I had to live with my mom at the age of 40."

In Proverbs 14:20 it says, "There is a way seem right unto a man, but at the end thereof are ways of death." This doesn't mean a physical death, but a type of death where there is no quality of life.

Steve said, "I remember we were sitting at your dinner table, and you asked me what I dream about. I couldn't answer the question. I knew then that I had to do some soul searching, and it had never occurred to me that my thought process was so messed up. I didn't realize that what I was thinking was affecting my entire life—I was unaware I had control over my thoughts."

I replied, "You have to be vigilant in your thinking because what you think about you bring about."

"It's so clear to me now," Steve replied. "Once you change your thought process, then you can create your life how you want it to be."

Philippians 4:8 says, "Finally brethren, whatsoever things that are true, whatsoever things are honest, whatsoever things are good, report; if there be any virtue, and if there be any praise, think on these things." Why should you think on these things? Because your life is a mirror or a reflection of what you think. As I stated earlier, good thoughts and bad thoughts are creating your own life.

CHAPTER 15: DREAMS

An involuntary vision occurred to a person while awake. Let's look at this word "involuntary" a little closer. This word means not voluntary; independent of one's own choice; unintentional; unconscious. This is why you have to pay close attention to the thoughts that go on in your mind. You can have some bad thoughts as well as some good thoughts unintentionally, not by your own choice, creep into your mind. If you decide to act on the thoughts, then you have just gotten what you dreamed.

I think a lot of people don't have the things they want in their life because they are unconscious or not aware in their thinking, so it makes me wonder if there could be a force stronger than what we all know, unconsciously controlling things and how they go. For this reason alone, an individual must be careful, attentive, and vigilant in one's own thinking. You must consciously choose good thoughts or, unconsciously, you will choose badly. Whatever you think about, you bring about.

I feel people have been getting everything they have been dreaming; I believe that they are not aware of the dreams inside their reality. The other morning I was on the computer, and I stumbled across something Albert Einstein once said: "No problem can be solved from the same level of consciousness that created it."

The End

ABOUT THE AUTHOR

Author Ruby Larry's personal entrapment in life's time wasting illusion is what ultimately inspired her to write this book. As she regained consciousness and became more aware of what is real, she was compelled to share her story so readers around the world could see what she saw and learn what she learned through her journey back to reality.

www.ingramcontent.com/pod-product-compliance
Lightning Source LLC
Chambersburg PA
CBHW070505100426
42743CB00010B/1765